SUPERCHARGE YOUR SOLID SURFACE BUSINESS

Save Time, Earn More, and Get Repeat Orders More than You Could Ever Imagine

SUPERCHARGE YOUR SOLID SURFACE BUSINESS

Save Time, Earn More, and Get Repeat Orders More than You Could Ever Imagine

GAURAV KABRA

Worldwide Published by
Pendown Press

PENDOWN PRESS

An ISO 9001 & ISO 14001 Certified Co.,

Regd. Office: 2525/193, 1st Floor, Onkar Nagar-A,
Tri Nagar, Delhi-110035

Ph.: 09350849407, 09312235086

E-mail: info@pendownpress.com

Branch Office: 1A/2A, 20, Hari Sadan, Ansari Road,
Daryaganj, New Delhi-110002

Ph.: 011-45794768

Website: PendownPress.com

First Edition: 2023

ISBN: 978-93-5554-626-5

Layout and Cover Designed by Pendown Graphics Team

Printed and Bound in India by Thomson Press India Ltd.

Dedication

This book, "Supercharge Your Solid Surface Business: Save Time, Earn More and Get Repeat Orders more than you could ever imagine," is dedicated with love to:

***Priyanka Kabra,** my beautiful wife and my best friend. Your unwavering faith in my dreams has been the north star guiding me through life's daunting challenges. Your love, strength, and resilience have been the foundation of our shared journey.*

***Aarav Kabra,** my energetic son. You carry the world in your curious eyes, and your youthful energy ignites in me a fire to be better each day. May you always chase your dreams as fiercely as you have inspired me to pursue mine.*

***Aarohi Kabra,** my bright daughter. You are the melody that brings joy to my life and the artist whose colors fill our home. Your creative spark has been an everlasting source of inspiration in this journey.*

Each of you have been my rock, my cheerleaders, my comfort, and my source of endless inspiration. Without you, this endeavor would have remained a mere dream. This book stands as a testament to your love, patience, and unwavering belief in me.

Thank you for being the centre of my world. This is dedicated to you.

Contents

Preface i

About The Book iii

Author Bio v

Who Should Read This Book? vii

How To Use This Book? x

Acknowledgements xii

Chapter 1

Understanding The Solid Surface Industry: A Primer 1

Chapter 2

The Production and Import of Solid Surface Sheets 8

Chapter 3

Staying Ahead of the Market: Trends and Predictions in Solid Surface 12

Chapter 4

Powering Up Your Solid Surface Business: Mastering Time Efficiency 15

Chapter 5

Maximizing Profitability: Strategies to Elevate your Solid Surface Business 19

Chapter 6

Increasing Efficiency in Inventory Management and Supply Chain 23

Chapter 7

Mastering Solid Surface Fabrication: Preparing for Perfection 27

Chapter 8

Revolutionizing Your Reach: Effective Marketing Strategies for the Solid Surface Business 30

Chapter 9

Securing Customer Loyalty: Winning Strategies for Repeat Business in Solid Surface Industry 33

Chapter 10

The Road Ahead: Future-proofing Your Solid Surface Business 37

The Author Closing Remark 41

Preface

Introducing "Supercharge Your Solid Surface Business: Save Time, Earn More, and Get Repeat Orders More Than You Could Ever Imagine." This book is the culmination of my years of experience, research, and passion for the solid surface industry. As an author and industry expert, my goal is to provide you with valuable insights and practical guidance to thrive in this dynamic field.

Within the pages of this book, we will embark on an enriching journey of exploration, starting with a strong foundation of understanding the acrylic solid surface industry. We will delve into essential topics such as production processes, market trends, pricing strategies, and supply chain optimization. Moreover, you will also uncover valuable insights on application techniques, marketing strategies, building strong client relationships, and fostering a culture of innovation.

Throughout the book, I encourage you to reflect on your own business practices and embrace new strategies for continuous growth. I am grateful to the industry experts who have generously contributed their expertise, enriching the content of this book. To you, the reader, I express my deepest appreciation for your time and trust. My sincere hope is that this book inspires you, provides practical guidance, and empowers you to overcome challenges, seize opportunities, and unlock the full potential of your solid surface business.

Join me on this transformative journey as we explore the world of solid surfaces together, paving the way for your success.

"Success is not final; failure is not fatal:
it is the courage to continue that counts."

~Winston Churchill

About The Book

"Supercharge Your Solid Surface Business - Save Time, Earn More and Get repeat orders more than you could ever imagine" is a comprehensive guide meticulously crafted to empower entrepreneurs and professionals in the solid surface industry. This transformative book delves into various aspects of running a successful solid surface business, providing practical strategies, expert insights, and valuable tips for maximizing profitability and achieving long-term success.

From understanding the fundamentals of the solid surface industry to exploring market trends and predictions, the book covers essential topics such as efficient time management, inventory management, supply chain optimization, and customer loyalty strategies. It also delves into the intricacies of solid surface fabrication, emphasizing the importance of perfection and quality in delivering exceptional products.

The book goes beyond operations and production, addressing the significance of effective marketing strategies to reach a wider audience and revolutionize business growth. Additionally, it provides guidance on future-proofing the business, highlighting the importance of embracing new technologies, fostering innovation, and adapting to the ever-changing landscape of the industry.

The author, having established his brand over more than a decade, shares his trials and triumphs throughout his journey in the industry. His aspiration is to connect with as many solid surface industry partners as possible, aiding them in their path towards achieving their ambitions. Expressing gratitude for the support he has received, he seeks to contribute positively to the industry and aid others in their journey of business growth.

Drawing from his extensive experience and the collective wisdom of his team, the author shares insights that can support those who share his dreams, ambitions, and goals. Ultimately, this book is an essential asset for both seasoned professionals and those new to the industry, providing the knowledge and tools to overcome challenges and seize opportunities in the solid surface industry. It is a testament to the author's commitment to contribute positively and meaningfully to the industry he's become a part of.

Author Bio

Meet Gaurav, India's first and only Solid Surface Growth Strategist. With over 18 years of experience in the building material industry, his unique and innovative strategies are helping professionals excel in the competitive solid surface industry.

Education & Qualifications

- Gaurav is a graduate in B-Com from Mumbai University.
- He holds certifications as an expert in Business Mastery Programme, Advanced Sales, and Overbooked Marketing Strategies.
- Notably, he is an expert in Business Operations Automation, demonstrating a flair for leveraging technology to optimize business processes.
- Additionally, he is a certified trainer in 'Spin-Selling' & 'Disc', testifying to his depth of knowledge in sales techniques and behavioral assessments.

Personal Information

Gaurav is "India's only Solid Surface Growth Strategist", setting a high standard for strategic thought leadership in the building material industry.

- With over 18 years of experience in the building material industry, he has amassed a wealth of experience working on a broad spectrum of projects and assignments.
- As a member of the Rs 4000/- Cr Entrepreneur Club, he has proven himself to be a collaborative growth member.
- He is a founding member of Granium, a well-known brand in the Indian Solid Surface market.
- Additionally, he holds a prominent position within the Rs 1000/- Cr diversified business conglomerate (HMB Group), which further testifies to his valuable insights gained into the dynamics of high-value businesses.
- Demonstrating an unparalleled talent for growing businesses, Gaurav has worked with over 800+ businesses and played a pivotal role in boosting their profits by 30% to an astounding 400%.

Gaurav's track record showcases an exceptional professional journey marked by continuous learning, practical application, and a relentless drive for growth. His accomplishments and expertise offer invaluable insights for those seeking to elevate their solid surface business strategy and operations.

Who Should Read This Book?

If you are a design enthusiast, an architect, a professional in the interior design industry, an entrepreneur, a business owner, a manager, or someone who appreciates the beauty of solid surface sheets, "Supercharge Your Solid Surface Business: Save Time, Earn More, and Get Repeat Orders More Than You Could Ever Imagine" is a must-read for you. This book offers valuable insights and inspiration for anyone seeking to explore the world of solid surface designs.

- **Designers and Architects:** For designers and architects, this book serves as a comprehensive guide and a source of inspiration. Discover the endless possibilities and creative potential that solid surface sheets bring to your projects. Learn about the craftsmanship, techniques, and innovative applications that can elevate your designs to new heights.
- **Interior Design Professionals:** If you work in the interior design industry, this book will deepen your understanding of solid surface sheets and their impact on spaces. Gain valuable knowledge about the durability, versatility, and aesthetic appeal of these materials, enabling you to make informed choices and create stunning interiors for your clients.

- **Solid Surface Artists and Craftsmen:** If you work with solid surface sheets and want to take your craftsmanship to the next level, this book offers invaluable insights and techniques. Explore the artistry behind solid surface designs, learn traditional and new techniques, and gain inspiration from experts in the field.
- **Entrepreneurs in the Solid Surface Industry:** If you own or manage a business in the solid surface industry, this book is your ultimate guide to success. Unlock strategies to streamline operations, attract new clients, and build long-term customer loyalty. Learn how to save time, increase profitability, and earn more repeat orders than ever before.
- **Business Owners and Managers in Related Industries:** Even if you're not directly involved in the solid surface industry, this book can provide valuable insights into optimizing your business processes. Discover innovative approaches to customer satisfaction, technology integration, and fostering growth that can be applied to a wide range of industries.
- **Anyone Seeking Inspiration and Knowledge:** Whether you have a professional background in design or simply appreciate the beauty of solid surface materials, this book will ignite your imagination and broaden your understanding. Gain a deep appreciation for the craftsmanship, versatility, and aesthetic appeal of solid surface sheets.

"Supercharge Your Solid Surface Business" is a comprehensive resource that caters to a wide range of readers. It offers practical advice, inspiration, and expert guidance to help you excel in the world of solid surface designs and drive your business to new heights.

Thank you for considering this book, and we hope it becomes a valuable companion on your journey to success in the solid surface industry.

How To Use This Book?

This book is a comprehensive guide for individuals in the solid surface materials industry who want to supercharge their businesses. Here's how to make the most of it:

- **Start by Setting Clear, Concrete Goals:** Identify your specific aims concerning time efficiency, boosting earnings, and securing repeat orders. Having a clear vision will help you focus your learning.
- **Strategic Reading:** Don't just skim through, instead, read with intent. Concentrate on chapters that address your priority areas, making sure to underline or highlight key concepts and principles that resonate with your objectives.
- **Take Detailed Notes and Reflect:** As you navigate through the book, jot down points that strike you as significant. Make it a point to reflect on these tips and strategies, considering how best to implement them in your own business context.
- **Create a Detailed Action Plan:** Don't leave the strategies in the book; bring them into your business. Break down the strategies into manageable steps, set realistic timelines, and create a roadmap to success.

- **Experiment, Evaluate, and Adapt:** Remember, not all strategies will fit your business perfectly. Be flexible and willing to adapt. Test out different methods and see what works best for you.
- **Measure Progress and Iterate:** Implementing changes is just the first step. It's crucial to evaluate the impact of these strategies, track your progress, and refine your methods as necessary.
- **Network and Engage in Continuous Learning:** Extend your learning beyond the pages of this book. Connect with other industry professionals, share ideas, and learn from their experiences.

Ultimately, this book is a valuable toolkit filled with insights and practical advice. By applying these principles, you can elevate your solid surface business to new heights. Embrace the journey of transformation, and get ready to supercharge your business.

Acknowledgements

Creating "Supercharge Your Solid Surface Business: Save Time, Earn More and Get Repeat Orders more than you could ever imagine" has been an enlightening journey, made possible by the unwavering support of numerous individuals. The threads of their love, faith, and encouragement have woven the tapestry of this work. I would like to take a moment to express my heartfelt gratitude to each and every one of them.

Firstly and foremost, I extend my heartfelt appreciation to my mother, Smt. Reena Kabra, a beacon of love, strength, and resilience. You have been my first teacher, my fiercest cheerleader, and my constant source of motivation. The values you instilled in me form the backbone of my life and work. The roots of this book can be traced back to the seeds of confidence and perseverance you sowed in me. This book is a tribute to your enduring faith in my dreams.

To my esteemed maternal uncles, Shri Ashok Bhaiya, Shri Arun Bhaiya, and Shri Anil Bhaiya, who have been sources of unending guidance, wisdom, and inspiration, I extend my heartfelt gratitude. Their invaluable insights, nurtured by years of experience, have not only enriched this book but also profoundly impacted my own life. I am fortunate to have had them as my guardians, mentors and strong supporters.

Additionally, I am deeply grateful to my Dealers and Fabricators, who have provided me with immense learning on this journey of success over the past decade. Their contributions have been invaluable in shaping my understanding and expertise in the field. Furthermore, I express my sincere appreciation to my Mentors, who have provided me with direction and guidance in executing this book.

The journey of creating this book has been an exploration of not just professional challenges but also of personal growth, and I am grateful for the unwavering support of the individuals who helped me navigate the rough waters. Their belief in my vision helped transform the concept of "Supercharge Your Solid Surface Business: Save Time, Earn More and Get Repeat Orders more than you could ever imagine" into a reality.

Thank you for holding my hand through this journey, and for being the wind beneath my wings.

Chapter 1

Understanding The Solid Surface Industry: A Primer

Origins and Evolution

The solid surface industry, a dynamic and transformative sector, has significantly impacted interior design and architecture. Tracing its origins back to the 20th century, the industry's breakthrough came in 1971 with DuPont's debut of Corian in the USA^, revolutionizing surface applications from healthcare to home interiors.

Initially, acrylic solid surfaces carved out their niche in countertops and healthcare environments. The material's seamless and non-porous nature of the material made it an ideal option for settings where cleanliness and hygiene were of utmost importance. Its durability, resistance to stains, and ease of maintenance made it an attractive choice for countertops, sinks, and various other surfaces.

As the years rolled by, the methods of manufacturing these solid surfaces underwent significant transformation. Advancements in technology enabled a broader range of colours, patterns, and finishes to became available, enhancing the adaptability of these surfaces. Additionally, innovations led to larger sheet sizes and increased thickness, thereby widening their scope of applications in both residential and commercial sectors.

Solid surfaces have undergone significant evolution, appreciated for their durability, stain resistance, and ease of maintenance. Over time, advancements in technology have diversified the options for colour, pattern, and finish, while improvements in manufacturing techniques have resulted in larger and thicker sheets, expanding their application range.

Versatility has been a key feature, with manufacturers harnessing the ability to mold and shape the material seamlessly. This opened creative avenues for architects, designers, and homeowners, and fueled competition among manufacturers, leading to higher quality products and reduced lead times.

Today, solid surfaces are prevalent in numerous settings-from countertops and sinks in homes to decorative elements in commercial establishments. Environmental considerations have spurred the development of eco-friendly surfaces, and digital technologies like CAD software and 3D carving are pushing the boundaries of design and manufacturing even further. As a result, the industry continues to experience robust growth, poised for a future driven by technological advancements and sustainability.

(Ref : A Brief History of DuPont Corian DuPont. 2013. Archived from the original on June 15th ' 2023 – via YouTube)

Properties and Characteristics

- **Non-Porous and Hygienic:** Acrylic solid surfaces exhibit a non-porous nature that resists stains, mold, and mildew, making them easy to clean. These attributes fulfill stringent cleanliness requirements, particularly in healthcare and laboratory environments.
- **Durability:** Known for their durability, as they can withstand impact, scratches, and heat, effectively retaining color and vibrancy, even under direct sunlight.
- **Seamless Appearance:** The seamless fabrication of acrylic solid surfaces enhances aesthetics and hygiene by eliminating crevices for dirt accumulation, easing cleaning, and maintenance.
- **Customizability:** Acrylic solid surfaces can be thermoformed into various shapes and forms, offering limitless design possibilities, both functional and artistic.
- **Colour and Texture Options:** With a wide range of available colours, textures, and finishes, these surfaces accommodate diverse aesthetic visions.
- **Repairability:** Their ability to be repaired and restored to original condition after minor damages makes them a cost-effective and durable solution.
- **Hygiene:** The non-porous nature of acrylic solid surfaces offers hygienic benefits by preventing the growth of bacteria, mold, and mildew. This makes them ideal for settings such as healthcare facilities and kitchens where cleanliness is crucial.

Overall, these characteristics contribute to the versatility of acrylic solid surfaces in different industries, from countertops to wall cladding.

Applications and Design Possibilities

- **Unleashing Creativity with Solid Surfaces:** Solid surfaces, with their unique properties, offer a broad canvas for designers and architects to explore. Primarily used in residences at kitchens and bathrooms, they have expanded their applications to include wall cladding, furniture, and even flooring in shower areas. This versatility and adaptability have unlocked new possibilities for creative expression.
- **Customizing With Solid Surfaces:** Solid surfaces thermoformability opens up design possibilities unmatched by natural stone or traditional materials, facilitating the creation of customized designs meeting individual preferences. This flexibility enables the creation of bespoke sinks, vanities, and even intricate temples designs.
- **Commercial and Public Applications:** Solid surfaces have significantly impacted the commercial sector, adding an element of elegance to reception counters, meeting tables, retail spaces, check-in counters, restaurants, and hotels. Due to their durability and low maintenance requirements, they are also widely used in public installations like transportation hubs and educational institutions, where their robustness is highly valued.

- **Looking Forward: Innovative Uses:** With ongoing innovation, the future promises evenmore inventive applications for solid surfaces, including integrated lighting, sensory surfaces, and art installations that push the boundaries of creativity. The design potential with solid surfaces is only limited by one's imagination, offering a functional and visually appealing design medium for various projects.

India Market Analysis & Drivers

Projected Indian Solid Surface Market Size (in Crores)

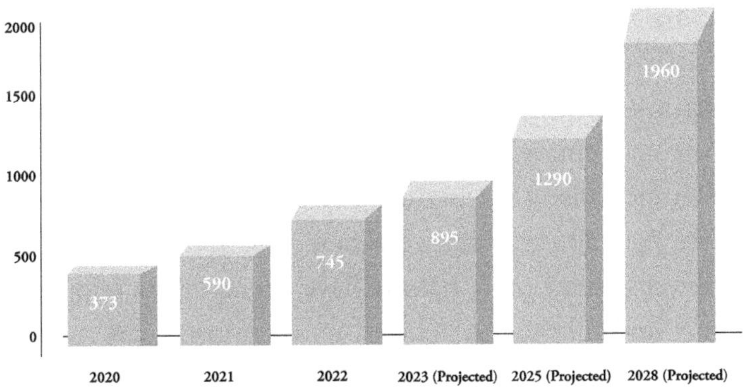

The Indian Solid Surface Sheets market is not only growing but flourishing, experiencing a remarkable 140% increase in market size within just three years. Projections indicate continued growth, with the market expected to reach a cap of Rs 1290 crores by 2025 and Rs 1960 crores by 2028. This represents a staggering 425% increase compared to the beginning of this decade. This upward trend demonstrates the tremendous potential for further value growth in the next decade or two.

Driving this growth are shifting consumer preferences, a strong commitment to environmental sustainability, and emerging design trends. Indian consumers are gravitating towards modern, hygienic, and durable interiors, making solid surfaces an ideal choice. These surfaces offer a sleek, seamless appearance, along with resistance to bacteria, and ease of maintenance, perfectly aligning with the contemporary aesthetic favored by many Indian consumers. Moreover, the industry's focus on sustainability is evident in the use of recyclable materials and the ability to repurpose surfaces, which resonates with the growing environmental consciousness among consumers.

India stands as a significant importer and user of this material, With the rising proportion of the upper-middle class having a keen interest in interior design, predicting a steady increase in demand. The construction sector's utilization of solid surface sheets further contributes to the thriving market growth. As major brands divert their attention towards research and development, new brands have an excellent opportunity to enter and fill the gap. Therefore, monitoring the market to identify and rectify deficiencies, as well as seizing the right opportunities, is crucial in this flourishing industry.

The Indian market analysis reveals opportunities for businesses to develop their brands and ensure long-term growth. Conducting comprehensive market analysis, including understanding market size, growth rate, potential customer segments, and competition, is crucial. These analyses provide valuable insights into customer behavior and emerging market trends, serving as a guide for strategic decision-making. By remaining adaptable, overcoming challenges, and capitalizing on future trends, businesses can maintain a competitive edge in this rapidly evolving market. Ultimately, the Indian acrylic solid surface industry, with its contemporary aesthetics, practical benefits, and emphasis on sustainability, presents significant growth prospects for businesses.

Chapter 2

The Production and Import of Solid Surface Sheets

The production and importation of solid surface sheets play a crucial role in meeting the increasing demand for these versatile materials. This chapter presents a thorough overview of the production processes along with the importation procedures necessary to fulfill market requirements. A comprehensive understanding of these aspects is essential for manufacturers, suppliers, and consumers operating in the solid surface industry.

Manufacturing Process

- **Raw Materials:** The production process begins with the selection of high-quality raw materials. Solid surface sheets typically consist of a blend of acrylic resin (MMA), natural minerals (ATH), and pigments. The quality and composition of these raw materials directly impact the final product's performance and aesthetic characteristics.

- **Mixing and Blending:** Once the raw materials are procured, they undergo a precise mixing and blending process. This involves combining the acrylic resin, minerals, and pigments in specific proportions to achieve the desired color, texture, and pattern. Advanced mixing techniques ensure uniform distribution and homogeneity of the materials.
- **Casting and Curing:** The blended material is then poured into molds or casts, where it undergoes a curing process. This process entails subjecting the material to controlled temperature and pressure conditions, allowing it to solidify and achieve its desired strength and stability. The duration of the curing process may vary based on the specific product and the manufacturer's recommendations.
- **Cutting and Finishing:** After the curing process, the solidified sheets undergo precise cutting into desired sizes and shapes using advanced cutting tools. The edges are carefully finished to ensure smoothness and uniformity. Techniques such as sanding, buffing, or polishing may be employed to achieve the desired surface finish.

Import of Solid Surface Sheets

- **Global Market Analysis:** The import of solid surface sheets plays a significant role in meeting the demand for these materials in the domestic market. Conducting a comprehensive analysis of the global market helps in identifying trustworthy suppliers, assessing market trends, and understanding pricing dynamics. Factors such as quality, pricing, delivery times, and sustainability practices should be considered when selecting import sources. The future of the solid surface materials market holds promise, driven by increasing construction activities worldwide, especially in emerging economies like India, and the growing demand for durable and visually appealing materials.

- **Supplier Selection and Evaluation:** Choosing the right suppliers is crucial to ensure consistent quality and reliable supply. Thorough evaluation should be carried out based on factors like product quality, manufacturing capabilities, certifications, and adherence to ethical and environmental standards. Building long-term relationships with trusted suppliers can foster mutual growth and contribute to the success of the business.
- **Logistics and Customs Compliance:** Efficient logistics management is essential for smooth import operations. This includes coordination with freight forwarders, handling customs clearance procedures, and ensuring compliance with import regulations and documentation requirements. Timely delivery and accurate paperwork are crucial to avoid delays and maintain an efficient and seamless supply chain.

- **Quality Control and Assurance:** Implementing robust quality control measures is of utmost importance to ensure that the imported solid surface sheets meet the required standards. This involves conducting thorough inspections, testing samples, and verifying compliance with specifications and industry benchmarks. Maintaining a robust quality assurance system is essential to provide customers with reliable and consistent products.
- **Compliance and Certification Requirements:** Solid surface sheets must meet certain safety, quality, and performance standards. These standards may include certifications such as ISO 9001 for quality management and ISO 14001 for environmental management. Additionally, they must adhere to safety regulations regarding fire resistance, chemical emissions, and impact resistance to ensure consumer safety. Importers have a responsibility to ensure that their suppliers provide compliant products and consistently uphold these regulatory standards to maintain product quality and safety.

Chapter 3

Staying Ahead of the Market: Trends and Predictions in Solid Surface

In the rapidly evolving world of interior design and construction, it is essential for professionals to stay ahead of the market and be aware of the latest trends and predictions. This holds particularly true for acrylic solid surface materials, which have gained immense popularity in recent years due to their versatility, durability, and aesthetic charm. In this chapter, we will delve into the emerging trends and predictions in realm of acrylic solid surface, offering valuable insights to help designers, architects, and manufacturers in navigating this ever-evolving industry landscape.

Innovative Design Patterns

- **Boundless Creativity:** Designers are embracing innovative design patterns that transcend traditional solid colours and simple patterns. This trend encourages boundless creativity, enabling exploration of unique shapes, geometric designs, and intricate organic motifs.

- **Advanced Technologies:** Manufacturers are investing in advanced technologies to create mesmerizing patterns. The introduction of 3D designs, grill designs, embossed patterns, and translucent layers brings depth, opulence, and a captivating interplay of light and material, enhancing the visual allure of solid surface materials.

Natural and Organic Inspirations

- **Replication of Natural Textures:** Solid surface materials have made significant advancements in replicating the vein patterns found in natural elements like stone, wood, and marble. Manufacturers have developed techniques to recreate intricate patterns and textures, offering a vast array of options that combine the durability of solid surfaces with the timeless appeal of natural materials.
- **Biophilic Design:** The incorporation of natural textures and patterns in solid surface materials promotes biophilic design, fostering a connection to nature and creating calming and rejuvenating spaces. This trend also aligns with sustainability initiatives and the use of eco-friendly materials further enhancing its appeal.

Integration of Smart Technologies

- **LED Lighting Systems:** Solid surface materials now incorporate embedded LED lighting systems, providing the ability to customize colours, create dynamic lighting effects, and serve as ambient lighting sources. This technology elevates the aesthetics and functionality of spaces, enabling personalized experiences and fostering immersive environments.

- **Touch-Sensitive Surfaces and Interactive Displays:** Solid surfaces equipped with touch-sensitive capabilities offer intuitive and interactive control, allowing users to adjust settings or activate functions with a simple touch. Additionally, the integration of interactive displays provides valuable information, entertainment, and engagement, further elevating the functionality of spaces.

Sustainability and Environmental Impact

One of the most influential trends shaping the solid surface industry is sustainability. In response to increasing consumer and corporate environmental consciousness, manufacturers are pioneering innovations that utilize recyclable materials and design surfaces with repurposing capabilities. Looking ahead, it is evident that sustainable practices and environmentally-friendly products will continue to drive growth and inspire innovation in the industry.

Demand for Hygienic Surfaces

Recent global events have sparked a sharp increase in the demand for hygienic surfaces, particularly in sectors such as healthcare, food service, and domestic sectors. Solid surfaces are exceptionally well-suited to meet this need due to their non-porous nature and resistance to bacteria, mold, and mildew. We anticipate that this emphasis on hygiene will persist, shaping the future trajectory of product development in the industry.

Chapter 4

Powering Up Your Solid Surface Business: Mastering Time Efficiency

In the fast-paced realm of solid surface businesses, mastering time management is a game-changer. The more efficiently you can manage your time, the more productive and successful your business becomes. This chapter unveils simple yet powerful strategies to help you save time, increase productivity, and supercharge your solid surface business.

1. **Quick Capture:** Quick Capture is a time management tool designed to swiftly jot down all your tasks. This single-point capture method reduces stress by ensuring tasks are not forgotten. It's crucial to transfer tasks from Quick Capture into your work system on daily basis. If tasks remain in Quick Capture for more than a day, it becomes a cluttered, stressful to-do list. Therefore, Quick Capture promotes efficiency, prevents overlooked tasks, and helps in stress reduction.

2. **The 80/20 Rule:** The 80/20 rule, also known as the Pareto Principle, states that approximately 20% of your

efforts results in about 80% of you. In terms of time efficiency, this principle emphasizes focusing more on the tasks that really matter and generate results. By identifying the most important tasks and dedicating the majority of your time to them, can accomplish more and benefit your business. This approach allows you to work smarter, not harder.

3. **Spot the Unnecessary Tasks:** Scan your day-to-day operations. Identify tasks that don't add much value to your business. Perhaps you're spending hours sorting paperwork or getting into the minutiae of planning. Could this time be better spent? You'll be amazed at how much time can be saved by eliminating or streamlining low-value tasks.

4. **Delegate with Trust:** Delegating tasks can feel overwhelming, as you may worry about the outcome meeting your standards. However, it's worth giving it a try! By entrusting 2% to 20% of your workload to your team, you can save time without compromising the quality of your operations. What's more, it can encourage your team members to grow and become more skilled.

5. **Magic of Scheduling:** Scheduling is the magic element of successful time management! Any task you want to get done should be scheduled with a specific start and end time. It's advisable to include a buffer of 15-30

minutes between tasks to account for any unexpected events. Your day can be divided into two parts: before and after lunch, and schedule repetitive tasks for the second half. Adopt a weekly scheduling approach: begin with your weekly schedule, ensuring recurring tasks are placed into the weekly planner, which will reveal the empty slots available. Remember, never start a week or day without a schedule. With all recurring tasks neatly placed in your weekly calendar, you'll have a clear and organized schedule that drives your productivity. What you schedule will Get Done, while what you don't schedule will Not.

6. **Magic of Batching:** Batching, or grouping similar tasks together, is a crucial time management strategy. Start by listing all your tasks spread throughout the day, week, or month, and then batch them based on their similarities. This approach minimizes the "switching cost," which is the time lost when transitioning between different activities or tasks, also known as the changeover cost. For example, you can batch tasks such as vendor, client, and staff meetings; documentation and report tasks including signing cheques, approvals, and report writing; follow-ups and coordination activities; and handling emails among others. By batching similar tasks, you can enhance your efficiency by reducing the time spent switching between different types of tasks.

7. **Parkinson's Law and Time Efficiency:** Parkinson's Law suggests that "work expands to fill the time available for its completion". In other words, if you allocate more time to a task, it tends to take longer to finish. To improve time efficiency, it's important to set specific and realistic deadlines for your tasks. By giving tasks the right amount of time, without excessive padding, you can boost your productivity and prevent work from unnecessarily dragging on. Understanding and implementing this principle is a key aspect of effective time management.

Chapter 5

Maximizing Profitability: Strategies to Elevate your Solid Surface Business

Profitability is the ultimate goal of any business, including those in the solid surface industry. However, achieving maximizing profitability goes beyond simply increasing sales. This chapter offers a set of strategic, practical, and effective approaches to boosting your bottom line and accelerating your solid surface business's growth.

1. **Smart Purchasing Practices:** Buying at the right price is crucial. Cultivate strong relationships with suppliers to negotiate favorable deals, such as bulk purchase discounts, or flexible payment terms. Consider joining buying groups to leverage collective bargaining power.

2. **Inventory Management:** Efficient inventory management can unlock capital and minimize storage costs. Implement a system to track your inventory levels, ensuring you have sufficient stock to meet customer demands while avoiding excess inventory. Consider using software tools to automate this process and enhance accuracy.

3. **Operational Efficiency:** Enhancing operational efficiency can lead to significant cost savings. Aim to minimize waste by streamlining processes, removing redundancies, and investing in automation wherever feasible. Remember, every minute saved equates to money saved.

4. **Value-Added Services:** Differentiate your business from competitors and provide additional value to your customers by offering services like custom cuts, installations, or after-sale support. These value-added services can attract new customers and allow you to command premium prices.

5. **Pricing Strategy:** Set your prices wisely. Pricing should not only cover costs but also reflect the value you provide, market trends, and what the competition is doing. Periodically review and adjust your pricing strategy as needed.

6. **Upsell, Cross sell & Re-sell:** Upselling involves encouraging customers to purchase a higher-end product or add-on features to enhance their chosen item. Cross-selling, on the other hand, aims to sell complementary products or services that enrich the main purchase. Lastly, reselling refers to the process of retaining customers and motivating them to make repeat purchases, which can be achieved through stellar customer service, loyalty programs, and regular customer engagement.

7. **Customer Retention:** Retaining existing customers is often more cost-effective than acquiring new ones. Focus on providing excellent customer service, implementing loyalty programs, and maintaining regular communication with your customers through newsletters or social media to maintain a loyal customer base and foster long-term relationships.

8. **Financial Management:** Keep a close eye on your finances. Regularly track your income, costs, cash flow, and profit. Use these numbers to guide your decisions. Keeping a sharp eye on your finances helps you spot problems early, make smarter choices, and boost your profits.

9. **Continual Learning and Innovation:** Stay updated with industry trends, new products, and emerging technologies. Continuously seeking knowledge and fostering innovation allows you to remain competitive and seize new market opportunities.

10. **Work Within Your Primary Competency:** Focus on what you're best at in your solid surface business. This may involve providing superior-quality materials, delivering exceptional customer service, or possessing unique technical know-how. By directing your energy towards these core competencies, you can impress customers, outperform competitors, and command higher prices. This approach not only saves time and resources but also enhances profitability and efficiency.

11. **Sustainability:** Modern consumers place a growing emphasis on the environmental footprint of their purchases. By offering eco-friendly alternatives and demonstrating sustainable business practices, you can attract a new demographic of customers and justify premium pricing.

12. **Training and Development:** Invest in your team's professional growth. Offering regular training and growth opportunities can enhance their skills, elevate service quality, and boost overall business productivity.

Chapter 6

Increasing Efficiency in Inventory Management and Supply Chain

Inventory management and supply chain efficiency are crucial elements in the success of a solid surface business. These interconnected aspects of business operations significantly impact profitability and influence various factors such as customer satisfaction and operational costs. This chapter aims to shed light on how to maximize efficiency in inventory management and streamline the supply chain.

1. **Understanding Inventory Management:** Inventory management is a systematic approach that encompasses sourcing, storing, and selling inventory— solid surface sheet, joint adhesive, and more. In the solid surface business, efficient inventory management can make all the difference between a satisfied customer and a lost one.

   Understanding your inventory means knowing what's in stock, where it is, and how quickly items move. This level of insight can be achieved with an inventory management system that provides real-time access to inventory data, thereby avoiding stockouts and overstocks and enabling better decision-making.

2. **Adopting Effective Inventory Control Techniques:** Several inventory control techniques can be applied to ensure effective management of inventory. The ABC analysis can be useful in identifying high-value items that require careful handling. Embracing the Just-In-Time (JIT) approach allows businesses to reduce storage costs by maintaining low inventory levels and ordering stock precisely when it is needed. Cycle counting, an inventory auditing procedure, ensures the accuracy and currency of inventory records, thereby facilitating seamless business operation

3. **Demand Forecasting:** Demand forecasting involves estimating the amount of stock required in the future. This might sound subjective, but with careful analysis of your sales data and market trends, you can make highly accurate predictions. Effective demand forecasting helps you in planning your purchases, preventing stockouts and excessive overstocking.

4. **Efficient Stock Rotation:** For solid surface materials that have a limited shelf life, stock rotation is essential. Prioritize selling your oldest stock first to prevent it from becoming unsellable. A well-organized warehouse can make this process streamlined and more effective.

5. **Implementing Efficient Supply Chain Mapping:** Supply chain mapping is a comprehensive process that identifies every component within your supply chain. It includes recognizing suppliers, manufacturers, distributors, and customers. Through supply chain mapping businesses can identify potential bottlenecks and areas that requires improvement, thus optimizing the flow of products from suppliers to customers.

6. **Building Strong Supplier Relationships:** Reliable and effective suppliers are vital to an efficient supply chain. Businesses must vet their suppliers for reliability, timeliness, and quality. Strong relationships with suppliers are built on transparent communication, fair negotiations, and timely payments. This foundation of trust ensures a steady flow of goods, thereby reducing the likelihood of interruptions in the supply chain. Furthermore, sharing vital information such as sales data and stock levels with suppliers fosters collaborative planning, minimizing waiting times, and ensuring the availability of the right items at the right time. This team effort not only cut costs but also make your supply chain more efficient.

7. **Making Transport and Logistics More Efficient:** Good transport and logistics get your products where they need to go quickly and cost-effectively. You can use software to plan the best routes, make loading and unloading faster and more efficient, and collaborate

with reliable logistics partners. This makes your deliveries faster, reduce costs and improves customer satisfaction.

8. **Leveraging Technology in Inventory Management and Supply Chain:** Modern technology offers valuable tools for inventory management and optimizing supply chain operations. Software solutions can automate tedious tasks, provide real-time inventory data, and deliver analytics for well-informed decision-making. Tools such as warehouse management systems, enterprise resource planning (ERP) systems, supply chain management (SCM) software or a simple inventory management system on excel or google sheet file too can significantly enhance efficiency in these domains.

9. **Fostering a Culture of Continuous Improvement:** Last but not least, successful businesses foster a culture of continuous improvement. Regular audits of inventory and supply chain processes serve to identify areas in need of enhancement. Performance indicators and metrics can be used to track progress and guide improvements. Additionally, feedback from employees, customers, and suppliers can also provide valuable insights for improving operations.

Chapter 7

Mastering Solid Surface Fabrication: Preparing for Perfection

Before Solid Surface Fabrication

- **Design and Planning:** Ensure you possess a clear understanding of the project requirements and design specifications before initiating the fabrication process. This includes accurate measurements, layout, and detailing.
- **Material Selection:** Choose the appropriate solid surface material that fulfills the project's aesthetic, functional, and performance prerequisites. Consider factors such as colour, pattern, thermoforming ability, thickness, and durability.
- **Surface Preparation:** Thoroughly prepare the substrate or existing surface by cleaning, leveling, and rectifying any imperfections. This ensures a smooth and even foundation for the solid surface fabrication.

- **Cutting and Fabrication Tools:** Choose the appropriate cutting and fabrication tools for the specific solid surface material being used. This includes selecting the suitable saws, routers, and other equipments required to achieve precise and accurate cuts.
- **Adhesive and Joining Techniques:** Determine the correct matching adhesive and joining techniques for the project. Also consider factors such as bond strength, curing time, and aesthetic requirements for seamless connections.

After Solid Surface Fabrication

- **Quality Control:** Conduct a comprehensive inspection of the fabricated solid surface components to verify they align with the desired specifications and meet the expected quality standards. Check for any defects, imperfections, or inconsistencies.
- **Finishing and Polishing:** Apply appropriate finishing techniques to achieve the intended surface texture and appearance. This may involve processes such as sanding, buffing, or polishing the solid surface material to enhance its visual appeal and smoothness.
- **Installation and Mounting:** Properly install and mount the fabricated solid surface components in accordance with the project's design and specifications. Ensure accurate alignment, secure fastening, and seamless integration with other elements.

- **Sealing and Maintenance:** Apply an appropriate sealant or protective coating to the fabricated solid surface to augment its durability, stain resistance, and ease of maintenance. Furnish the end user with detailed instructions on proper care and maintenance to ensure its longevity.
- **Customer Satisfaction:** Prioritize customer satisfaction by engaging in effective communication, promptly addressing any concerns or issues, and providing post-installation support and maintenance guidance. Procatively seek feedback to continuously improve your fabrication processes and services.

Chapter 8

Revolutionizing Your Reach: Effective Marketing Strategies for the Solid Surface Business

In the competitive solid surface industry, effective marketing and promotion play a vital role in distinguishing your brand and captivating customers. This chapter delves into the strategies and techniques that can assist you in marketing and promoting your solid surfaces effectively. From understanding your target audience to establishing a strong brand presence, we will explore various aspects of marketing that can contribute to the success of your business.

1. **Identifying Your Target Audience:** Before formulating any marketing strategy, it is crucial to identify your target audience. By understanding the needs, preferences, and demographics of your potential customers, you can customise your marketing efforts to resonate with them. Conduct market research, analyze customer data, and create buyer personas to gain valuable insights into your target audience.

2. **Building a Strong Brand Identity:** Establishing a strong brand identity is paramount for differentiation and recognition in the solid surface industry. Craft a compelling brand story, a distinctive logo, and visual elements that reflect your unique value proposition. Consistently convey your brand message across all marketing channels to create a memorable and consistent brand image in the minds of your customers.

3. **Online Presence and Digital Marketing:** In the digital era, a robust online presence is crucial for marketing success. Build a user-friendly website, optimize it for search engines, and leverage social media platforms, email marketing, and online ads to expand your reach to a wider audience. Develop informative content to establish your industry expertise. Maintain organized data, use WhatsApp bots for efficient customer support, and provide comprehensive product information and catalogs to potential customers, ensuring they have access to the information they need.

4. **Showcasing Your Work:** Visual representation plays a vital role in marketing solid surfaces. Develop a compelling portfolio of your best projects, showcasing the versatility, beauty, and quality of your work. Utilizing high-quality photographs, videos, and case studies can be powerful marketing tools to demonstrate your expertise and captivate potential customers. Consider participating in trade shows, exhibitions, and

industry events to exhibit your products and forge connections with professionals in the field to expand your network.

5. **Building Relationships and Networking:** Networking plays a significant role in the success of any business. Actively attend industry events, become a member of professional associations, and engage with architects, interior designers, contractors, and other industry key stakeholders in the solid surface industry. Building strong relationships with these individuals can lead to valuable referrals and collaborations, expanding your reach and credibility within the solid surface industry.

6. **Customer Testimonials and Reviews:** Positive customer testimonials and reviews have great power to influence the decision-making process of potential customers. By encouraging satisfied clients to provide feedback and share their experiences, you can make a significant impact on your business. Display these testimonials prominently on your website and marketing materials to build trust and credibility.

7. **Continuous Improvement and Adaptation:** Marketing is a dynamic and ongoing process that demands continuous evaluation and adaptation. It is crucial to monitor the effectiveness of your marketing efforts, track key metrics, and make data-driven decisions accordingly. Furthermore, it is important to stay updated with the latest marketing trends and emerging technologies in the industry to remain competitive and relevant.

Chapter 9

Securing Customer Loyalty: Winning Strategies for Repeat Business in Solid Surface Industry

In the highly competitive solid surface industry, one of the fundamental keys to your business's growth and sustainability lies in customer retention. Securing repeat orders not only ensures a consistent flow of revenue but also fosters strong and lasting relationships with your clients. This chapter aims to explore practical strategies that can help you to build trust and loyalty among your customers, ultimately leading to an increase in repeat orders.

1. **Delivering Quality Products Consistently:** Quality is a non-negotiable aspect of the solid surface industry. Maintaining high-quality standards is crucial for preserving customer trust and loyalty. This means working closely with manufacturers and suppliers to ensure the quality of the solid surfaces you distribute. Regular product inspections and quality checks should be part of your operations to prevent any potential

issues or sub-standard products from reaching your customers.

2. **Maintaining Reliable Delivery and Stock Availability:** Reliable delivery and consistent stock availability are of utmost importance in the solid surface distribution business. Ensure that your supply chain and inventory management systems are robust and efficient enough to minimize stockouts and delays. By consistently meeting delivery times and ensuring an ample stock of popular products, you can establish a reputation for reliability, which in turn makes customers more likely to place repeat orders.

3. **Providing Excellent Customer Service:** Excellent customer service is vital for securing repeat orders. This involves promptly addressing customer inquiries, efficiently resolving issues that may arise, and providing reliable after-sales support. It is crucial to ensure that your customer service team is well-trained to handle various situations and maintains a courteous and professional demeanor. Investing in customer service can significantly enhance customer satisfaction and loyalty.

4. **Establishing Transparent Communication:** Maintaining transparent and regular communication with your customers can greatly boost their trust in your business. Keep your customers well-informed about any alterations in pricing, product availability,

or delivery schedules. In case of any issues or delays, proactively communicate with your customers, clearly explain the situation, and propose a viable resolution. Transparency in communication can reinforce customer trust and foster a stronger business relationship.

5. **Building Personal Relationships:** In the business-to-business (B2B) sector, personal relationships play a significant role. Grab the opportunity to attend industry events and trade shows to establish face to face connection with your customers. Personal interactions like these can help in building stronger connections and nurturing loyalty. You can also consider organizing customer appreciation events or send personalized messages or gifts on special occasions.

6. **Keep in Touch with Customers:** In the solid surface industry, securing customer loyalty extends beyond delivering quality products. A significant strategy is to maintain regular contact with customers through personalized communication. This can involve sending festive greetings or sharing valuable product knowledge that can benefit them. Additionally, educating customers on relevant industry and business topics can facilitate their growth, indirectly contributing to the success of your business. Such targeted and personal interactions not only reinforce your dedication to customer satisfaction but also make clients feel valued, encouraging repeat business and loyalty.

7. **Providing After-Sales Support:** After-sales support, including installation guidance, maintenance advice, and warranty service, can make a profound impact on customer satisfaction and build loyalty. Providing comprehensive after-sales support shows your unwavering commitment to customer success, even after the sale is completed.

8. **Soliciting and Acting on Customer Feedback:** Seeking customer feedback serves as more than just a method to assess customer satisfaction; it presents a valuable opportunity to enhance your services. Encourage customers to provide feedback, both positive and negative. Act on this feedback promptly, making necessary improvements, and proactively inform the customers when their feedback has driven positive changes. This practice demonstrates the value of their opinion, thus making them feel appreciated and more likely to place repeat orders.

9. **Implementing a Customer Loyalty Program:** Customer loyalty programs can serve as a powerful method to encourage repeat orders. Such programs can manifest in different forms, including discounts on future orders, implementing points-based systems, or exclusive benefits for repeat customers. A well-structured loyalty program can offer customers with tangible incentives that motivate them to maintain long-term relationship with your business.

Chapter 10

The Road Ahead: Future-proofing Your Solid Surface Business

In today's rapidly evolving business environment, it is crucial to pro-actively future-proof your solid surface business in order to ensure long-term success and sustainability. This final chapter delves into essential strategies and practices that will empower you to navigate the road ahead and maintain a competitive head.

Personal Preparedness

Before embarking on your solid surface business journey, it is crucial to ensure personal readiness. This entails being physically, emotionally, and financially prepared to confront the challenges of entrepreneurship. Thorough preparation and learning in advance can prevent counter productivity and lay a sturdy foundation for your business. Always remember, perseverance is key to long-term success.

Focus on Problem-solving

As the leader of your business, it is crucial to tackle one problem at a time and make well considered decisions. You serve as the driving force behind your business, and your ability to remain calm and focused will serve as an inspiration for your team. By addressing challenges systematically, you can uphold stability and foster a productive work environment.

Comprehensive Understanding

Develop a comprehensive understanding of all aspects of your business to set realistic expectations for yourself and your employees. Acquiring knowledge of different functions and operations within your business will facilitate effective management. By avoiding knowledge gaps you can streamline workflow, minimize decision-making time, and foster seamless functioning throughout your organization.

Supply Chain Clarity

Achieving clarity in your supply chain and establishing a well-defined hierarchy within your organization is essential for long-term sustainability. It is vital to define roles, responsibilities, and workflows in a clear manner to facilitate efficient and effective operations. Proper division of work, coupled with a well-defined supply chain, minimizes decision-making time and promotes seamless functioning.

Quality Over Price

While the appeal of low prices may drive initial sales, emphasis on quality is imperative for long-term success. Providing cheap products may lead to negative customer experiences and damage your business reputation. It is essential to prioritize delivering high-quality products that align customer expectations, as this fosters trust and cultivates a positive brand image.

Strategic Profit Margins

Take careful consideration of market dynamics when setting profit margins. Identify the strength of your business, such as competitive pricing, unique products, strategic positioning, or prime locations. Understanding your advantages over competitors will enable you to set appropriate profit margins and lead in the market.

Embracing People and Technology

In today's highly competitive world, technology plays a crucial role in gaining a competitive edge. However, it's essential to recognize that the success of any company lies in its people. While technology enables efficiency, it's the collective efforts, collaboration, and empowerment of individuals that fuel sustainable growth. By emphasizing on cultivating a culture that values its workforce, encouraging innovation, and leveraging technology to enhance human potential, solid surface businesses can effectively compete and flourish in this dynamic environment. It's through the seamless integration of people and technology that secures a resilient future for the industry.

Power of Continuous Learning

In a rapidly evolving business landscape, embracing continuous learning is essential for achieving success. Learning extends beyond traditional classroom settings and certificate programs; it involves equipping your workforce with the necessary skills to adapt to future jobs requirements.. As technology advances and new challenges arise, it becomes essential for solid surface businesses to identify skill gaps, foster a culture of learning, and enable employees to acquire new knowledge. By embracing a growth mindset and nurturing a culture of continuous learning, businesses can remain agile and thrive in an ever-changing industry.

Reflecting Your Values

Your personality reflects in the products and services you offer. It is essential to ensure that your products meet the expected quality standards, as customers can draw conclusions about your responsibility and reliability based on their experience. By upholding high standards, you can elevate your brand's reputation and establish strong partnerships for future growth.

The Author Closing Remark

In conclusion, I want to extend my heartfelt appreciation for accompanying me on this journey to enhance and expand your solid surface business. I trust that the insights and strategies shared in this book have empowered you to unlock the full potential of your enterprise.

Throughout my decade-long journey in the solid surface business, I have collaborated with numerous designers, dealers and fabricators. Capturing all of these experiences in a single book is indeed challenging.

My mission in life is to empower my partners in the solid surface industry. My ultimate goal is to assist you to exponentially grow your business, achieve financial independence, and assist you in carving a fulfilling life. To bring this mission to life, I am ready to schedule a one-on-one meeting with you, where I would introduce you to additional strategies for heightened profitability that would ultimately contribute to a more joyful life.

To schedule our meeting, please don't hesitate to contact me via email at: gaurav@granium.com. When you contact me, kindly reference the title of this book to help me better understand your objectives and ensure our conversation is productive and focused.

Additionally, I invite you to connect with me on LinkedIn at: https://www.linkedin.com/in/gaurav-kabra-99a02a45, where I regularly share valuable insights, industry updates, and strategies to solve industry challenges to fuel business growth.

Best regards,

Gaurav Kabra

Author and Solid Surface Growth Strategist.

"जो लोग बदलाव से नहीं डरते,
वे ही इतिहास बनाते हैं।"

NOTES: ✍

NOTES:

NOTES:

NOTES:

www.ingramcontent.com/pod-product-compliance
Ingram Content Group UK Ltd.
Pitfield, Milton Keynes, MK11 3LW, UK
UKHW021655190726
13853UKWH00001B/268

9 789355 546265